"Adventures in Adversity"

Surrounded by Angels

Autobiography By:
James S. Bernard
March 2010

"For He Shall Give His

Angels Charge over thee,

To keep thee in all

Thy ways"

PS.91:11

Contents

Contents

<u>Forward</u>

As I write my "Adventures in Adversity" I am approaching my 80th birthday. I wrote it for at least a couple of reasons. First, to take a mental review of my life (Perhaps for selfish reasons). Next to share the joys and sorrows the laughs and tears, the true "Adventures in Adversity" that I've experienced in these almost eighty years with you who are about to review my "Adventures in Adversity", truly surrounded by angels.

My sincere wish is that you will profit from my errors and benefit from the knowledge that there is a living Lord, whether you acknowledge him or not. He is there! I'm not sure how it all happened, but one thing I do know, in all my adversity I've been surrounded by angels and a living, loving Lord.

Early Childhood

I was born on April 9, 1930, in Eugene, Oregon at Sacred Hearts Hospital. We lived on East 21st Street in Eugene right next to the University of Oregon campus. As a young lad my Father would have me march behind the University of Oregon's band as they did their practice before an upcoming game. My Father, Arch Bernard, was Manager of the Mutual Life of New York. My mother, Beatrice, was a very committed home maker, although prior to marriage she had taught school in the Oregon City area. Strange as it may seem I do recall my 1st birthday, a cake with only one candle and all. I had an older sister Audrey Ann and a sister, Merrilu just a year younger than me.

These were the depression years, but we lived in a very attractive though not large home, and we did have an almost full time maid "Desee DeLong". I can recall hungry vagrants coming to our door asking for food or money which either "Desee" or my mother would oblige. Our mother, who for whatever reason we always called "Beela", would frequently make cream of wheat cereal for our breakfast. One morning after Audrey Ann had eaten and left for school, Merrilu and I were playing with our spoons with much remaining, now cold 'cream of wheat cereal' trying to figure out how to get rid of it. Sitting on the floor near the door out to the garage was a pair of Mrs. Byron's galoshes left by oversight after an evening bridge party at our home. Spotting them, aha! A perfect spot for our cold "cream of wheat". Quickly before our mother returned, we filled Mrs. Byron's galoshes with our remaining cereal. We never heard what the outcome was when Mrs. Bryon attempted to put on her galoshes again.

We always ate together as a family for dinner. After dinner my Father loved to tilt his chair way back and finish his coffee or enjoy a cigarette. However, one night he apparently tipped his chair back too far and crashed through the lead glass bay window and fell several feet below to our driveway. Fortunately, he was not seriously hurt, but our concern as children wasn't with his possible injuries, but the potential of burglars coming in through the now broken bay window.

As a family we attended the Episcopal Church. Father White was the priest. One time Father White took my sister Merrilu and me to our first circus. One Sunday in my Sunday school class the message or lesson was based on: Matt 21:22:

'Everything You Ask in Prayer, believing, you shall receive'. I guess the message stuck because that night after my mother tucked me in bed I said, "my now I lay me down to sleep" and she kissed me and left. I couldn't wait to put my Sunday school lesson to work and although I was approximately five years old it is as clear to me now as it was then.

My father was on a business trip to North Bend, Oregon and due home later that night. Out of no where after I had prayed believing 'Lord you know that what I've always wanted is a pocket knife'-a clear vision came to me of my father in his hotel room checking all the drawers before leaving finding a pocket knife, next thing after sleeping soundly I was awakened in the morning and heard my father describe exactly as I had envisioned his finding the knife to my mother. Right away I almost panicked because I thought how am I going to act surprised when he brings it to me? as a permanent reminder that God answers even the believing prayers of a small lad. I was playing with my knife and the blade accidentally closed on my right index finger leaving a scar that is yet visible seventy-five years later. God does answer prayer.

The Fall of my 5th year I was anxious to start first grade at Edison Grade School but they refused my entry because I wouldn't be six years old until April. By the time the next year rolled around I had become probably too attached to my mother and sister, Merrilu. My mother took me to my first day of school and left. No sooner had she left then I made a frightened exit and ran all the way home. My mother had to take me back two more times before I finally stayed.

On Mothers Day our first-grade class each made Mothers Day cards for our mothers. They were supposed to read "to my mother with love" but because I called my mother "Beela" I printed "to my Beela". The teacher made me cross it out and put "to my mother". On the way home I crossed "mother" out and printed above it "Beela".

I can remember about this time a newspaper boy coming down the street hollering "Extra! Extra! Wiley Post and Will Rodgers Crashed" and not too much later on a trip to Sunset Beach on the Oregon coast hearing on the radio about the missing "Amelia Ernhardt".

One Christmas time my father thought he should do, the outdoor thing and go to the woods to cut down our own Christmas tree. We all anxiously awaited his return. Several hours later he returned almost exhausted with the tree but

OCCASION FOR MANY

—Kennell-Ellis pho

Above is a typical scene to be enacted in many homes of Euge
Christmas morning. Pictured here are the children of Mr. and
Arch A. Bernard, gathered around the Christmas tree, busy wi
toys that mark such an occasion. At left, Audrey Ann, eight
in front is Jimmie, four years old; and in back, Mary
years old.

when my sisters and I saw the tree we all began to cry. Instead of our usual Douglas fir, it was a pine tree with pinecones. My father looked at his three crying kids, started to swear and dragged the tree out to the garbage followed by a trip to the tree lot and returning with our usual Douglas fir.

During the Christmas season MacMorn and Washburn, our largest department store, featured my sister Merrilu and me clad in night jumpers playing with toys in one of their feature windows and a picture of us in the Register Guard followed.

I was first introduced to fishing by my father. We had a cabin on the McKinsey River. My father would take me with his guide, the famous 'Prince Helfreg' to a spot several miles up stream from our cabin. There we would launch the drift boat and fly fish down stream to our cabin landing 18 to 20 native rainbow trout. Real fighters! By the time we reached our cabin my mother would have a fire going on the outside grill near the water. After cleaning the trout we would have breakfast by riverside of fresh trout and eggs. Yum! Yum!

During the summers often times our evening meal would consist of huge portions of strawberry short cake heaped with fresh whipped cream, boy was it good! Our father's parents

lived in Schenevus, New York and each year they would send us a one-gallon tin of real maple syrup. During the winter when we had snow, our mother would heat the maple syrup, and we would pour it over some fresh snow and it would make a great treat.

Backing up a little, in 1934 our whole family traveled by train from Eugene, Oregon to Schenevus, NY stopping at the Worlds Fair in Chicago. We stayed at the Palmer House in Chicago.

My best friend in Eugene was 'Dickie Hopkins'. Later when our family moved to Portland Dickie and I had an opportunity to take a flight in an open cockpit bi-plane. We were both tucked snuggly into the front cock pit and the pilot in the rear one. How excited we were with the flight. We each swore we would become aviators. As close as I came, at age fourteen, I took flying lessons in a piper cub until I had run out of money.

In the 1937 to 1938 we moved to the N.E. area of Portland where I attended Alameda Grade School. In late 1938 my father bought an unfinished home on five acres in Garden Home which is in S.W. Portland.

The Garden Home Gang

Pre Teen/Teen Years

In Garden Home my sister, Merrilu, and I attended Garden Home Grade School, my older sister Audrey Ann Tigard High School.

In addition to a large garden, apple trees and four cherry trees, my father decided to raise chickens (he was still in the insurance business). So we had over 1,000 chickens and all of us participated in caring for the chickens and preparing the eggs for market. We supplied the Original Pancake House with eggs and sold them at our farm for 39 cents a dozen. After the chickens had several diseases, my father decided to abort the chicken operation.

In the old chicken house after it was cleaned up I set up my radio and electrical shop. I had always had an interest in these areas. I would make and sell chystle sets. I also made two spark coil transmitters, one for me and one for Harry Feldman who was about my age and lived several miles down Garden Home Road. I strung an antenna up in our apple trees. We both learned the morse code and commenced transmitting back and forth. One day a big black newer car went back and forth in front of our home finally coming to the door they were the F.B.I. and said that our transmissions had been picked up hundreds of miles off the Pacific coast and that because we were now at war it was illegal and ordered us to dismantle them, which we did.

In my chicken house shop I set up a system so that when the front door opened (to the shop) it would ring a bell and I had placed a bucket of water attached to a small fan motor over the entrance, wired to a push button at my shop desk. When the door would open the bell would ring. I would then push the button to activate the motor to turn the bucket upside down dumping the water on the person entering. I was sitting at my shop desk hoping I'd have a chance to see my new system work. The bell rings! I push the button and hear a large crash and a big scream. My father had come in and the entire heavy contraption had fallen down on his head.

When I was about ten years old, I had an attack of what was thought to be appendicitis. I was taken to the old St. Vincent's Hospital, turned out not to be appendicitis after all but Dr. Adams probably to earn his fee took my appendix out anyway.

I was in the hospital for ten days. You can't believe how naïve I was. I heard a young patient yelling from the next room "nurse! Nurse! I've gotta take a shit!" I had to ask my mother what 'shit' was.

It was now in the early 1940's and our nation was at war. Several of the kids our age decided to form sides and have our own war. Our side had bee bee guns and when the other side made their attack at our farm, they only had sling shots so we, battering them with bee bees causing them to let out yelps and make a hasty retreat. However, within the hour they returned with reinforcements armed with bee bee guns which forced our side to retreat into one of our barns. Unfortunately, I opened a dirt and dust covered window to see where the opposition were. At that moment Jack Godwin stuck his bee bee gun close to my head and fired. Blood started gushing from my eye. My two sisters carried me to our home and I was taken to the doctor's office, where a bee bee had just missed my right eye and was removed.

On special occasions my father would take me on business trips. He had taught me to drive, although I was only about eleven years old. So, when he got tired I would take the wheel which was quite a treat for an eleven year old.

One time on a trip to Coquille, Oregon my father was to give a speech to the Kiwanis Club. As he was dressing shortly before the speech the zipper of his trousers failed and couldn't zip them up. After some panic he sent me to the dry cleaners where repairs were made in time for his speech. That afternoon I went with the son of one of my father's clients, while he delivered newspapers. One of the deliveries took us to an upstairs apartment where there were scantily clothed woman lining the stairs. I was to learn later that it was a 'brothel'.

When I was some where between twelve and thirteen years old I had saved up over $75.00 dollars from my early morning Oregonian route which was enough for me to purchase my first car, a 1930 Model 'A' Coupe with a rumble seat. During these war years gasoline, along with shoes and sugar was rationed. For pleasure use you received an 'A' sticker which only allowed you four gallons a week. You got a 'C' sticker which allowed you much more if you drove to work taking passengers. Needless to say I had only an 'A' sticker which when I ran short of fuel necessitated after dark ventures with my sister Merrilu, a rubber hose and a five gallon can to ers flew on strip in Coquille, Oregon. Once my father was to give a speech to the Kiwanis Club. As I was dressing shortly before the speech the zipper of his trousers failed and couldn't zip them up. After some time he rushed to the dry cleaners where repairs were made in time for his speech. That afternoon I went with the son of one of my father's clients.

when I ran short of fuel necessitated after dark ventures with ...... Harris, a rubber hose and a five gallon can to ......

provide fuel for my model 'A'. We would spot a car in a darkened driveway, and we would take turns on 'look out' and 'siphoning'. I'm sure we each must have swallowed a lot of gasoline. We'd come home with it on our breaths.

About this time my father had started taking the bus from Raleigh Hills to his work in Portland in order to conserve fuel. My mother would take him to Raleigh Hills, and I would on occasion be asked to pick him up. He had a newer 1939 Ford V8 sedan. I had been used to, in my model 'A' turning off the key coasting down hills to save fuel. So, at the top of the hill leading down to the Raleigh Hills junction I turned off the key and suddenly realized that it had locked the steering, and I was heading off the road to the right for a large tree, no way to avoid it. I crashed into the tree. When my father got off the bus all he saw was his totaled car surrounded by all kinds of concerned people. I thought that he would be furious, but instead he was grateful that I had only minor injuries and instead of punishing me he bought me new tires for my Model 'A'.

My sister and I would usually go on a Friday night to the movies either at the Joy Theater in Tigard or the movie theater in Multnomah. Some where about this time I met

thought was my first love. Ruth Stoops, a twin with a sister Ruby. In those days most parents never gave their children any explanation about sex. In fact, our parents gave us the impression it was a dirty subject. Needless to say, my romance with Ruth blossomed almost as naively as Brooks Shields in Blue Lagoon.

Mrs. Stoops, Ruth's mother must have been either very permissive or naïve herself because on several occasions I would spend the night with Ruth in her bedroom. Although no intercourse at this point a very exciting and interesting way to spend an evening.

I graduated from grade school in May of 1944 and started my freshman year at Tigard High School in the Fall of 1944. My sister Audrey Ann was already a senior by this time so before my first day as a freshman she chose my wardrobe, Levis and everything that was 'cool'. During my first days at Tigard High all the girls just 'swooned' about me and I felt like a movie star. I was nominated for Freshman Class President. All the girls voted for me but not the boys. I lost to a 'Red' O'Hallowen. Kind of a boy's boy. I turned out for football but during one of the first practice sessions I was tackled and

knocked briefly unconscious and carried off the field. I weighed only about 120 pounds so ended my football career.

About this time my romance with Ruth Stoops ended. I started skipping school and smoked about a pack of cigarettes a day. In Portland at 6th and Yamhill there was a 'Blind Street Vendors' stand. I would walk up and in a very deep voice say "a pack of Luckies please" and have no problem getting cigarettes.

My first experience with alcohol occurred when my father would take me into a tavern and order us each a glass of beer. It was legal in those days. However, that soon ended. However, as a family we were having lunch in Multnomah, my father ordered he and I each a beer. I apparently had gulped the beer and immediately threw up all over the table.

My father died in early January 1945. That night we could hear him yelling in extreme pain and then silence. I saw a bright flash of light as though it was his spirit ascending to heaven. He was gone.

My mother had sometime earlier gone to work at Esco Steel Foundry in the office so we children were left alone most of the time. I went through a very difficult period seldom attending school. One day Howard Hanson, the brother of Bob Hanson who married my sister Audrey Ann, brought a bottle or two of whiskey to our home and several of us started drinking. Eventually we all got in the Model 'A', some in the rumble seat with bee bee guns and drove up and down Garden Home Road shooting at windows, people you name it, finally returning to our home. Howard, the only one over eighteen years of age was in the shower when the police arrived. They hauled him off to jail but left the rest of us saying they'd be back. Fearful of what might happen, Bill and I took off in the Model 'A', our destination California and then Mexico. When we reached Sherwood, we ran out of gas. Nearby was a green newer Chevrolet four door and we checked it out and sure enough the keys were in it. We hopped in and took off on Highway 99 for the coast.

Later we'd discover that the car belonged to Nell's Anderson, our principal, at Garden Home Grade School. What a coincidence. There was also lots of gas rationing coupons in the glove box. By the time we reached the coast it was very dark, highway slippery. Somewhere near Hecetta head South of Yachats we lost control of the car on a sharp turn and went through the guardrail and were left hanging over a cliff with the ocean over a thousand feet below. Not knowing how long the car would remain before falling cautiously we exited the vehicle and proceeded on foot spotting a dump truck parked further down the road. Found the keys in it and drove it until it ran out of fuel. We then hitch hiked all the way to San Fernando, California on the way selling a valued watch to buy food. Our venture ended when Police found us sleeping in a San Fernando hotel lobby. They contacted Bill's parents and my mother. His father took the train down to pick us up. We remained in Jail. We returned by train with Bill's father. We then appeared before Judge Long and were placed on some kind of probation.

My wild times continued. By this time my mother had sold the property in Garden Home, and we'd moved to a small upstairs apartment on N.W. Thurman Street in Portland. My sister Merrilu and I attended Lincoln High School. One of my friends at Lincoln was Eddy Eben who was also possessed with a devilish spirit. We skipped school and went in search of a car to steal. On Broadway, not far from Lincoln High School, we found a newer red Pontiac two door coupe with the keys in it. It was wintertime. Some where near Maupin we spotted on a hillside a large unoccupied truck. We pulled behind it and found the rear door unlocked and low and behold when we opened the door it was filled with cases of whiskey. Why it had been left and unlocked is anyone's guess. We off loaded a case of Canadian Club keeping a bottle to drink. We hid the remainder up on the hillside behind some sage brush. After consuming a good portion of the bottle we proceeded on toward Maupin. It didn't appear to be icy but apparently it was. I was driving and attempting to negotiate a turn at a good rate of speed the car slid sidewise and then rolled over three times before coming to a stop upright. The top was so caved in I had trouble getting out. Eddy had been thrown from the car and was lying in the ditch. Neither of us were seriously injured, just bruised and some cuts. We were thankful to be alive. Believe it or not the car was still drivable. Some where in or near Maupin we found a Model 'A' with the keys in it, abandoned the Pontiac and off for Portland in the Model 'A'. We were traveling at a fairly high rate of speed as we approached Portland. A police car turned its' lights on and started to chase us. The chase went on for quite some time in one street out another almost tipping the model 'A' over. Finally on a fatal move we made a turn into a dead end street. Arrested and then again to Judge Long who for whatever reason released me to my mother.

Sea Going Years

By this time my blessed mother and sister were ready to do anything to get me off their hands. My mother had to pay for two wrecked vehicles in addition to all the, 'heart ache'. On my sixteenth birthday my mother took me to the Police station at 2nd and Oak where I received my first driver's license. I had been driving since I was eleven always very cautiously, but now since I was licensed, I felt a new freedom and proceeded to get three traffic citations on my first day with a license.

I was too young for any of the military services but old enough with my mother's consent to join the Merchant marines, which I did and on approximately May 10th of 1946 I sailed from Portland on the seagoing tug the 'Great Isaac'. My mother and sister were at the dock when I sailed and probably thought 'whee'! He is off our shoulders. The majority of the crew of the 'Great Isaac' were older seasoned sailors like 'Suit Case Larson' and a 'Popeye'.

We were sailing for Panama to escort two fishing vessels back to San Diego, the sea was calm, weather warm and beautiful.

We stopped for fuel in Acapulco which then was just a sleepy little fishing village. Although it did have a hotel on the cliff overlooking the harbor. I went ashore that night and after drinking too much in a small canteno woke up on the dock in the morning sun shining on my hung over body.

We reached panama a couple days later. I went ashore with several others and proceeded again to drink too much. I remember getting in a cab outside the drinking establishment but there was no driver. Finally in my near drunken stupor I got into the driver's seat and took off apparently down a one way street the wrong way. I heard police whistles and then gun shots. The next glazed my right hand but missing my head and blasting the windshield into thousands of pieces. Needless to say, I had stopped by this time. I was treated for my wounds and taken to the most God awful filthy smelly prison you could ever imagine. There were no beds, no chairs, only a wet slimy cement floor with dirty creepy men all standing or laying on the floor. I finally fell asleep on the damp cement floor. The next morning, I was taken to court. It was a very dark day with bolts of lightening and rumbles of thunder, as I write this it is still very vivid in my mind. My sentenced was read to me in Panamanian, the only thing in broken English that I understood was 250 days.

Led back to prison I was suicidal not knowing how long I'd be there or how I could end my life. I just gave up. I don't know how many days I was there, perhaps five. In deep remorse I heard what sounded like my name being called out 'James Bernard'. I was in a fog and didn't answer at first and then I stood up and looked near the entrance to our cell block and it was the 'purser' from the 'Great Isaac'. I don't recall if I cried in disbelief or whatever, all I know was that I was free. The Purser had to pay quite a fine to get me out and said they had all but given up on finding me and were prepared to sail. I hadn't earned enough to pay for my fine so they gave me extra overtime to offset it. We escorted the two fishing vessels back to San Diego. On the way we fished and landed a marlin, also a giant sea turtle.

From San Diego we sailed north to San Francisco where our voyage ended. I didn't have enough money for the train fare home, so the crew took up a collection for me. Arriving home I signed up at the S.U.P. hiring hall awaiting another ship. I purchased a 1932 Studebaker Dictator '8'. It was a black four

door sedan, lots of power. One night after probably drinking too much, four of us were driving wildly through the downtown streets of Portland when finally, a Broadway cab forced us over. He hopped out of the driver's side leaving the drivers door open and started for my driver's side. Before he could get to me, I put my car in gear and took off tearing his driver's door off. He some how got in the cab, door torn off and started chasing us. After some dramatic pursuit we lost him. I immediately drove to my mother's apartment which was in S.E. Portland and hid my car in her garage as it had sustained some damage.

I made many voyages during the next five years to China, Japan, Philippines, Formosa, Alaska, Mexico, Central and South America, Puerto Rico, through the Panama Canal, up and down the east coast. These sea going days were filled with excitement and adventure. Almost sinking in an outrigger off a Philippine Island, transporting, by 'Breeches Buoy' a crewman with a ruptured appendix from our ship to the hospital ship 'Mercy' in rough seas. Escaping, from a group of Chinese 'thugs', in Shanghai, China and much more.

Starting out as an Ordinary Seaman, then Able Bodied Seaman and finally as a Third Mate. During one of the

St. Johns Bridge

477°E (http://stable.toolserver.org/geohack/geohack.php?pagename=St_Johns_Bridge&params=45.58508_N_-122.76477_E_type:landmark)
From Wikipedia, the free encyclopedia

The **St. Johns Bridge** is a steel suspension bridge that spans the Willamette River in Portland, Oregon, USA, between the St. Johns neighborhood and the northwest industrial area around Linnton. It is the only suspension bridge in the Willamette Valley and one of three public highway suspension bridges in Oregon.[1]

The bridge has two 408 ft (124 m) tall Gothic towers, a 1,207 ft (368 m) center span and a total length of 2,067 ft (630 m).[2] The adjacent park and neighborhood of Cathedral Park, Portland, Oregon are named after the Gothic Cathedral-like appearance of the bridge towers. It is the tallest bridge in Portland, with 400 ft (122 m) tall towers and a 205 ft (62 m) navigational clearance.[3]

By 2001, average traffic on the bridge was 23,800 vehicles/day.

History

St. Johns Bridge

Carries	U.S. Route 30 Bypass
Crosses	Willamette River
Locale	Portland, Oregon
Maintained by	Oregon DOT
Design	Suspension bridge, Art Deco
Total length	2,067 ft (630 m)
Longest span	1,207 ft (369 m)
Clearance below	205 ft (62 m)
Opened	June 13, 1931
Coordinates	45.58508°N -122.76477°E (http://stable.toolserver.org/geohack/geohack.php?pagename=St._Johns_Bridge&params=45.58508_N_-122.76477_E_type:landmark)

At the time of the proposal to build the bridge, the area was served by a ferry which carried 1000 vehicles a day. The proposal for a bridge was initially met with skepticism in Multnomah County, since St. Johns and Linnton were over five miles (8 km) from the heart of the city, and local business owners had minimal political clout. But after a lobbying effort that included a vaudeville-style show performed at grange halls and schools throughout the county, voters approved a $4.25 million bond for the bridge in the November 1928 elections.[4] Initially a cantilever bridge was proposed, but a suspension bridge was selected due to an estimated $640,000 savings in construction costs.[5]

The construction of the bridge began a month before the Stock Market Crash of 1929 and provided many county residents with employment during the Great Depression.[6] Because of its proximity to the Swan Island Municipal Airport, some government officials wanted the bridge painted yellow with black stripes. County officials waited until St. Patrick's Day 1931 to announce that it would be painted green. [7]

Dedication of the bridge was put off for one month in order to make it the centerpiece of the 23rd annual

Maritime strikes I worked with a friend, Rueben Roth, painting the St. Johns Bridge in Portland. The pay was great. First we spent days painting inside the towers with three gallon buckets of paint, painting the inside. The fumes from the paint would make us delirious. During our lunch hour we would catch pigeons and take them home and cook them for supper. Our final day we were high up on scaffolding powered by an electric motor painting on the exterior of the arches. All of a sudden something failed, and my side of scaffolding started to fall. Seeing our problem the police were called and they stopped bridge traffic while full of fear, we were able to nurse the faulty scaffolding to the bridge surface. We went directly to the job shack, quit and collected our final checks.

About this time, I met my wife to be, Cherie Ann Miller who also attended Lincoln High School. Blonde, green eyes a real cutie with the cutest nose. We were married on January 1st, 1949, in Stevenson, Washington. We lived in a darling one-bedroom home in S.E. Portland. I continued my seafaring life. Most of our early meals consisted of macaroni and cheese (Kraft's) from a box or Spam with a red catsup sauce. One day when I returned from the Seaman's Hiring Haul Cherie informed me that a salesman was coming to demonstrate and sell us cookware. I said "no way"! We were in the kitchen with the lights out when there was a knock at the door. I said "Cherie, quick to the floor" he continued to pound on the door yelling "I know you are in there" and he started around for the kitchen door. Hurriedly we crawled on our stomachs to the front room. Finally, he gave up and left.

Our first son, Kristen, was born on October 19, 1949. While waiting for his birth I got so sick I went outside and threw up on the lawn.

To My Little Son

November 4, 194

The day that you, my son, were born,

I, your father, was surely worn,

I paced the floors I hopes, of views,

Or even a whisper of the news,

Without any luck,

A Cigarette I struck,

And Smoked and smoked,

Until I choked.

The nurses walked past,

And I thought,

Will I last?

The hands on the clock,

Seemed never to move,

I felt like hollering,

Let's get in the groove-

The people would look at my worried stare,

As if they thought,

I'd been treated unfair.

When the clock read

One-Thirty-Five,

You my son,

had finally arrived.

And the joy that filled my heart,

Far exceeded the thought,

That I'd soon have to part.

So now you'll know how ragged and torn,

Your daddy was,

The day you were born.

-Your loving Father-

Within a few days after Kris's birth, I left on a ship for New York and then Mobile, Alabama where the ship was layed up and the crew dismissed.

TO MY BELOVED WIFE
November 2, 1949

I'll always Love you, Cherie dear,

With all my aching heart.

You've been my everything,

Since the very start.

While in the far lands of Peru,

My heart beats strong for only you.

And in the distant land of Japan,

My heart ached more then

I could stand.

And now I've sailed away again,

To return, I know not when.

But while upon the seven

Seas I roam,

My only thought is you,

Our son, our home.

So I thought I'd write this rhym,

While in the passing of my time,

To let you know that

Whether far or near,

I'll always Love you, Cherie dear.

Your loving Husband,

-Jim-

We were given travel money to get home. I got four of my crew mates to give me as I recalled $100.00 each with the understanding, I would buy a car and we'd drive home. I went to a used car lot in Mobile and bought a black 1940 Packard Limousine, which had probably been either a funeral car or a gangsters. It had a roll up window separating the driver's area from the rear seats. It was real sinister looking. I paid $350.00 dollars for it. All excited about my purchase, I drove back to the ship to pick up my passengers. When I reached the ship, I tried to put it in reverse and the engine stalled, the battery was dead and one of the crew yelled out your gas tank is leading. I had the car towed to a small garage where an older black mechanic worked on the generator and transmission for more than seven hours. His bill was only $18.00. I gave him $25.00 and left. I picked up my passengers and headed for home. The car had no license plates, and it had a 'free wheeling' (since outlawed). When you took your foot off the accelerator it went out of gear. The steering was so loose you had to drive fast just to maintain steerage and the only way we could stop the leaking gas tank was to rub the holes with a bar of soap. When we pulled into a gas station, we had to keep the engine running to avoid it not restarting. Consequently, attendants were afraid to come out and wait on us. Five, unshaven men, in a black limo with the engine running. Finally, we'd get out and coax them to fuel us.

I was afraid to let anyone else drive because of the steering so I drove us three days with only two hours sleep all the way to Portland, Oregon.

I was so grimmey from my trip I stopped at a mobile station near our home to cleanup a little. The owner became very indigment and asked me to leave.

It was always such a treat and a thrill to come home to my wife Cherie and our son Kris.

I put an ad in the paper to sell the Packard. A peg legged fellow from Alaska came and paid $350.00 for the car. As he left I had to lift his peg leg on to the 'gas pedal' and he was off to Alaska. He gave me a call from Seattle and said he had the steering checked and only a small 'cotter pin' had kept the steering from going totally out.

About 1950 we had a chance to buy a new one story pumiced stone home at 9010 N.E. Eugene Street. It had two bedrooms a fireplace and an oil heater.

About Us | Services | Our Fleet | Photos | Safety | Careers | Contact Us

Grain

Ship Assist

Harbor Services

Power & Experience Working for You

Since 1880, Shaver Transportation has served clients of the Col
River system. Our success and reputation are built on our power
fleet and experienced people. Shaver services include ship assist
inland grain/bulk commodity barging and harbor services.

During another Maritime strike I got a job as a deck hand with Shaver Transportation Company. Oh, how I hated this job. It required that I had to hook up log rafts with a tow line to the tug. It was wintertime. I have a very poor sense of balance. The job required that I walk out on the slippery boom logs although I had calked boats. I would fall in the cold Willamette River at least once a day coming home each night with at least one set of soaking clothing.

In 1951 I was on a ship in Alaska which was then a war zone. Cherie was pregnant with our 2nd child. When I had returned to Seattle, I called Cherie to see how the pregnancy was progressing, the child wasn't due for several weeks. To my great surprise she said the baby had already arrived. I ran back to the ship all excited telling the crew our 2nd child had arrived. They asked was it a boy or a girl? I said by golly I forgot to ask, ran back to the phone and called Cherie who said "it's a girl". She had tried to contact me in Alaska but because it was a war zone no contact could be made. I hurriedly got a hair cut, bought a stuffed toy and flew home to me my new daughter, Kimberly. In December of 1951 our entire little

family Cherie, Kris, Kim and I traveled to Alameda California for me to attend the Merchant Marines Officers Facility. The training included Navigation, Rules of the Road, Semaphore, Seamanship communicating in Morse code, First Aid and much more. We rented a nice apartment in Alameda. In the evenings Cherie would help me practice semaphore which is communicating with two signal flags.

We had invited Cherie's mother, Mildred, over for Christmas dinner. Cherie among other things had prepared one of my favorites, a bowl filled with whip cream and fresh fruit. I knew her mother was a big eater and loved it too. So, I had Cherie hide it in the back of the refrigerator. When her mother arrived, what did she do? She went immediately to the refrigerator and pawed around and found my whip cream and fruit and started helping herself to it. Bless ole Millie!

I graduated from Officers School in late January 1952. While the knowledge I had acquired was still fresh in my mind I was anxious to get back to Portland to go before the Coast Guard to take what usually was five days of exams to receive my 3rd Officers (3rd mates) license. So, we left Alameda late in the afternoon and drove up the coast highway. We drove all night me first then Cherie. I went in for my exam on Monday morning and finished in record time on Wednesday and received my 3rd Mates License. I then had to join the union which is the Masters Mates & Pilots Union. I already was a member of the S.U.P. Sailors Union of the Pacific and the Inland Boatsman Union. It was at this time we were at war in Korea. When I went to the hiring hall I could take my pick of ships. There were more ships than officers to fill them. I picked the "S.S. Augustine Daly", a Liberty ship just out of the moth ball fleet being refitted for action.

The Saga of the S.S. Augustine Daly

I sailed from Portland, Oregon in early February 1952 on the Augustine Daly as Third Officer. It was well after dark when our ship was near Skemokawa, Washington (which means "Smoke on the Water") and true to form we were traveling at slow speed in dense fog. I was on the bridge along with the Captain, Pilot and Helmsman, all of a sudden out of seemingly no where we collided with a French Motor Vessel which had some how anchored in mid channel. All you could hear was the grinding of our hull meeting theirs. Neither vessel sustained damage endangering sinking. Because of the damage to our ship we returned to Portland, Oregon for repairs. What a surprise for my wife, Cherie, back already? Repairs took over ten days and in late February 1952 we again left Portland for a destination we'd later receive in secret orders; it would be Pusan Korea. After crossing the Columbia River bar, we sailed over calm seas and beautiful weather in a SWterly direction. The second day at sea the Bos'n was found dead of apparent natural causes in his bunk. Normally the body would be sewn in canvas filled with iron shackles and a burial at sea. But because of the uncertainty of his death, he was placed in the ship's freezer.

Beautiful weather and calm seas continued for several days, but something very strange was happening. The barometer which is a predictor of storms took a dramatic drop way down to 27:00. The Captain, a young Italian on his first voyage as Master thought our barometer was faulty and asked Sparks, the Radio Operator to contact other ships in the area to check their barometers, but no response.

Early the next morning all hell broke loose, winds had built up to over 120 miles per hour and when I came on to the bridge and saw mountains of seas rising well over 100 feet coming at us, my inner being was filled with fear. In five years of sea time I had never seen or heard of seas like this. The ship would rise into the sea going almost straight up, like climbing a mountain and then dive straight down on the back side. Finally, one high sea completely covered the ship with a high crash. I was in the chart room making an entry in the ships log and it knocked the original type of ink pen from my hand. The sea had cracked the hull ahead of the wheelhouse structure, washed part of the deck cargo overboard, smashed the life boat I was in charge of and washed it overboard. The Captain ordered Sparks to radio our position and that we had sustained considerable damage and could be in danger of sinking. The fear was so great among all the crew that few ate anything. I was almost paralyzed with fear, couldn't sleep as the gigantic storm continued. Finally in total desperation I got on my knees in my cabin and prayed (as I write this, tears come to my eyes). "Father forgive me for my sinful life, please save me and our ship. I promise I will change my way of life and seek to serve you all the days of my life". The storm continued for another day, but I was given a warm feeling of peace. What we had encountered was a typhoon out of the South China Sea. Many smaller vessels had been lost and many lives. When at night fall we reached the harbor of Pusen Korea, the wind was still howling. The Captain said drop the port anchor but the wind and current were so strong the port anchor chain parted and the Captain then said drop the starboard anchor which finally held. The ship had taken on a lot of water; lost most of the deck cargo, ventilators smashed in, lifeboat missing, hull cracked and had a large port list. It made such a sad looking sight that the Pusan paper featured a picture of the ship on its first page. Our cargo was unloaded, and repairs were made to the ship. We all thought that we'd be returning to the U.S. shortly but then like a bomb shell had dropped we learned that we would be shuttling ammunition from Japan to Korea for possibly as long as a year. At night we could hear U.S. bombers flying over on their way to North Korea and then we'd hear the thundering sounds of the bombs as they hit their targets. By late April poor Cherie was writing to me saying that she was lonely and missed me and when was I coming home?

Finally, an idea came to me, for which I had to ask the Lord's forgiveness. I wrote to Cherie and said if you want me home, send me a telegram saying the following: "your wife Cherie is very ill request you return home immediately signed your loving Mother". I guess I kind of forgot about it and one noon I was sitting in the Officers salon finishing my lunch, I felt a hand on my shoulder, it was the Purser. He said, "Jim, I have some bad news, your wife is very ill and they want you to come home". I was elated but I thought Jim if you ever needed to act now is the time. He continued by saying the Captain wants to see you right away. When I met with the Captain he said: "I suppose you want to go home" I responded "if it were your wife Captain wouldn't you want to go home?" So, he agreed to let me go, but getting out of a country at war is no easy task. I had to go through the Red Cross, the Korean Military, it was a real hassle. Finally with all the documentations my airlines tickets, which cost well over a thousand dollars, I boarded a Korean Airlines DC3. The plane was about to take off when a group of armed Koreans ran toward the plane, and they had me get out of my seat and rechecked my papers and left. What a scare! We took off flying over the mountains of Korea for Tokyo, Japan.

ill and request my return Home
immediately — if you do — I
could show it to the skipper
and ask that I be paid off
over here — it would only
take me about 20 hours —
less than a day to fly home.
— Its O.K. with me if you want
to try it. — the sooner Im
Home with you for keeps the
better. — You might word
the telegram as follows:
"Chris seriously ill. request
your return Home immediately"
                    Love mom.
tell them at the telegraph office   ....., calif.
that its an emergency message
— that may speed it up a little.
I will acknowledge it by a
message to you — saying Im

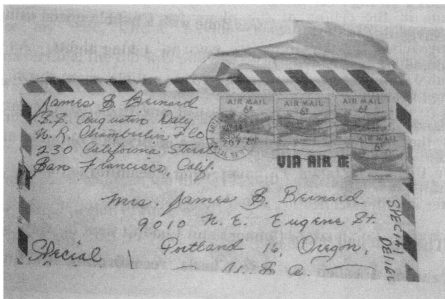

James B. Bernard
S.S. Augustin Daly
N.R. Chamberlin & Co.
230 California Street
San Francisco, Calif.

VIA AIR M:

          Mrs. James B. Bernard
          9010 N. E. Eugene St.
          Portland 16, Oregon,
               U. S. A.

Special

SPECIAL DELIVERY

I had corresponded with my wife's brother, Miles Miller, who was in the army stationed in Tokyo and he'd agreed to meet my plane. We met and went to a military bar for a beer and then back to the airport where I boarded a Canadian Pacific DC4. You could still see an almost faded P.A.M. on the fuselage as it had apparently previously been a Pan American plane. As I looked around the plane all the rest of the passengers were Chinese. In fact, the name of the plane was: 'The Spirit of Hong Kong'. After the plane was airborne, they commenced serving dinner, fish heads and bowls of rice. I thought, oh great. But when they got to me, they brought me a beautiful filet wrapped in bacon and a large baked potato. The plane was heading for Vancouver, BC with a stop in the Aleutians for fuel.

Navigating in those days was done with a bubble sexton using a dome in the ceiling of the plane for taking sights. As we approached the Aleutians, we were in a big snowstorm but landed safely, fueled and resumed our flight to Vancouver, B.C. As we crossed the west coast of British Columbia, and I saw the Douglas firs I thought 'what a beautiful sight'!

The flight had taken 17 hours, and I hadn't slept for day. After landing I called my wife Cherie, reconfirming my time of arrival in Portland. I took off in another DC3 for Seattle.

In Seattle I boarded the newest plane United Airlines flew, a DC6B. Shortly after getting airborne emergency lights came on, aboard we had a top U.S. General, it may have been "Bradshaw" I'm not sure. The plane had either been sabotaged; at any rate the engines weren't functioning right. The pilot got on the speaker advising us of making an emergency landing. As we approached the landing strip, I could see emergency ambulances and fire trucks with their lights flashing. I thought of all I've been through to end up crashing only a couple of hundred miles from home. What a sad way to go. However, we made a safe landing and were immediately put on another plane to Portland. When I got off the plane in Portland I got down and kissed the ground and swore that I would never go to sea again. As I got up I could see my wife, Cherie waving from our 1948 Chevrolet convertible, the top was down as it was a beautiful sunny day. We had been apart for almost four months. What a joy to be come! Cherie was as beautiful, if not more so than ever, and we drove up to the top of Rocky Butte where we were finally alone. You can imagine the love and passion after being apart for such a period of time.

Business Years

I had some important decisions to make. My income as a 3rd Mate in a war zone was huge, then about $2500 a month. I had to find a job soon. I started to work in the Bargain Room at Ward's. Forty dollars a week plus sales bonus's which didn't amount to much. Our weekly grocery budget was $10.00. I hadn't forgotten my commitment to serve the Lord, but was waiting for direction but take a look how 'God works in mysterious ways his wonders to perform".

My mother, Bee, by now was working at Edward Hines Lumber Company in Westfir, Oregon and lived in a duplex. In the other side of the duplex was the Presbyterian minister, Lyle Knaupp, who had just recently become the pastor at Roseway Presbyterian Church only a few miles from our home. At the same time Fred Thornton, an insurance salesman for North America Life & Casualty Company whose manager was Paul Knaupp, Lyle's brother. Fred had called on us following up on birth notices. Long story short, Bee asked Lyle Knaupp to call on us and we subsequently started

attending his church. Fred encourages me to meet Paul which I did (Paul also a Christian) and subsequently I started working part time for North America Life & Casualty Company. Soon I was making more money part time selling insurance than I was at Ward's. So soon I was selling insurance full time, my manager Paul Knaupp a Christian and going to Roseway whose minister was Paul's brother, Lyle Knaupp. Our agency secretary was Hazel McElfish, a dedicated Christian. Talk about God sending his angels! These folks made a dramatic difference in my life.

At Roseway, where we attended church every Sunday, Cherie taught in the nursery and I taught initially, the junior boys and then the adult class. On several occasions I filled the pulpit delivering the sermon and conducting the service.

Our third child, Bradley Shawn, was born on October 28, 1953. Our fourth child Barbara Ann was born three years later on November 17th, 1956.

Most of our summers, we went camping in the Bend area and to the Oregon Coast. Thanksgiving we'd travel to Cherie's folks in San Francisco and Spring Break to Palm Springs.

On one of our trips to San Francisco for Thanksgiving traveling in our Ford Country Squire I had Barbara sitting in the rear seat which face to the rear with binoculars keep a lookout for the police. We would leave Portland in the early morning, and it would take us approximately ten hours traveling at over the speed limit to reach San Francisco. On that particular trip Barbara had missed spotting a police car and we got a ticket. Poor Barbara started to cry thinking she had let her Dad down.

In 1958 Cherie and I were traveling with our new minister, Bob Harvey and his wife Marjorie to the Rose Bowl where Oregon was playing Ohio. Nearing Pasadena we had been eating 'bourbon balls' which are made with 'booze'. It was New Year's Eve and as we approached a roadblock, where the police were checking for drinkers we thought how funny it would be if a minister and his elder got arrested for eating 'bourbon balls' on New years Eve. Oregon put up a good fight but lost 10 to 7.

I continued with my insurance career receiving my C.L.U. designation in 1961 after four years of classes.

I had so many wonderful experiences with Paul Knaupp. On one occasion after our workday in insurance, still in our suits and ties we drove to the Cowlitz River to fish for steelheads. We'd cast our lines with cherry bobber out into the Cowlitz, put our rods into rod holders and got back into the car to keep warm. All of a sudden, I noticed my line moving, Paul said 'oh it's just moving on the bottom'. Then I saw my rod come out of the rod holder and a large steelhead diving out of the water on the end of my line. By the time I got to my rod it was out in the water. I jumped into the water, suit on and all now up to my waist in the water and grabbed my rod. The fish made another big leap, what a fish! But oh no, coming down stream was a large log between me and the fish and 'snap' went the line and the fish was gone and I was soaking wet and cold.

On another occasion Paul had invited me to join him at this duck club. It was still quite dark as we crawled with our guns toward the duck pond. Paul said quietly 'now don't shoot until the birds start to fly', but I guess Paul got a little anxious and seeing the ducks on the pond started shooting. Only problem, they weren't ducks but decoys and Paul had destroyed several decoys.

One night as we were having dinner with two other couples, we started talking about the 'Roaring Twenties', a live theater show near the train depot. Very popular, but because of the crowds, it was almost impossible to get into. I said "let me see what I can do". I had a white Thunderbird with red leather interior and a red phone. I called the 'Roaring Twenties' and said "This is Sir James I'm approaching Portland in our private jet we've heard about your establishment, could you make arrangements for the six of us we'll be arriving in a white Thunderbird and gold Cadillac. "Oh yes Sir James! We'll be happy to accommodate you". We drove up to the Roaring Twenties entrance and two valets took care of our cars. People were all lined up behind a velvet cord waiting to get in. The person in charge took us through the crowd, opened the velvet cord and led us to prime front row seats. Hence forth I've been know as 'Sir James'.

The insurance business continued to prosper, now having branched into all lines of insurance. We bought a new split-level home at 9285 SW Washington Street where we lived from 1959 to October of 1975. Most of our memories with raising our children took place here. Up until this time I had been

spending most of my evenings calling on prospective insurance clients. Now I was able to be home most evenings.

One of our neighbors was Shreve Carter whose son was Bobby. Bobby loved to trout fish. He had never been salmon fishing so one fall Saturday, Shreve, Bobby and I took Shreve's small open boat and went salmon fishing on the Columbia. Bobby had his small trout rig we had our salmon gear in the water along with Bobby's. We'd been fishing for over two hours with no action. Finally, Bobby looked at his Dad in disgust and said "salmon fishing is such a bore"! No sooner had the words come out of his mouth and a twenty-pound salmon struck his line. Talk about a zoo. We were all about dozing off, the fish had almost spooled Bobby's small reel. We had to chase the fish finally landing it. "Dad, salmon fishing is such a bore"! Not anymore!

In 1974 we bought a quarter acre lot on Bull Mountain and built a 4500 square foot home with three fireplaces, a sauna, a bar, wine cellar and a pool. By the time we moved into our home in October of 1975 the children were all married or close to it.

With Kris and Brad, my sons, we had a great adventure in a variety of business ventures. In addition to the insurance operation a premium finance company, a Century 21 franchise, a candle factory, construction company, a country western restaurant, West by NW Marine Sales, considerable real estate holdings including the Clackamas Professional Plaza, a mini shipping center, duplexes, single family rentals, apartments, condos in Hawaii, investments in gold and silver. Some very exciting years! We made lots of money and lost a lot but I wouldn't change the experience for anything.

During the Carter Presidency there was very high inflation and high interest rates. There was considerable speculation. We, my son Kris and I, had done considerable building individual houses, fourplexes and the Clackamas Professional Plaza. We had purchased almost an entire block in Clackamas which consisted of a large warehouse, a mini shipping center, a large two story home and vacant land. As I recalled we only paid $175,000.00 for it. We sold the warehouse for over $200,000.00, the shopping center, for $350,000.00 and the lot for the Clackamas Professional Plaza for $100,000.00. We moved the house to a lot we owned and sold it for $75,000.00.

Adding it up:

$200,000.00	Warehouse
$350,000.00	Mini Shopping Center
$100,000.00	Lot
$75,000.00	Home
$725,000.00	
175,000.00	
$555,000.00	Profit (over ½ million)

As I recall we did this all with less than $50,000.00 invested. Quite a return!

However, when Regean became President in 1982 he immediately put the brakes on the economy and lending dried up. Many of our projects had been sold on short term contracts to be refinanced within two years. When that time came there were no funds available to refinance. Hence our construction loans to Equitable Saving and Loan, Oregon Mutual, U.S. Bank and others went in default which ultimately resulted in all but U.S. Bank going under.

We started getting sued from all directions, process servers banging on our door's night and day. We could have wall papered an extra home with the legal papers we were served. We were in the process of making an orderly disposition of our assets when several of our creditors thinking that we were

hiding assets, in November 1982 forced a very unusual 'Involuntary Bankruptcy' which meant that all of our assets were liquidated at only a few cents on the dollar. In terms of real value, we had a net hard equity of well over 2,000,000 million dollars.

At one point Kris and I each had in addition to our other vehicles New Subaru S.W. Vince Williams the Subaru Dealer gave me a call and said "the hook was out for Kris's Subaru. But unfortunately, when the hook came, he took my Subaru instead of Kris's.

Backing up a bit, we had built a new building at S.E. 42nd and Divison. Our insurance operation on one side and we leased the other side to Century 21. The real estate operation wasn't doing very well so they asked if we'd be interested in purchasing it which we did for only $8500.00. Within two weeks an old listing sold for a commission almost equal to our purchase price.

During our bankruptcy I had only a very limited income. On my mornings jog I would pick up cans and usually I would sing "it's a ten can morning Lord" "it's a ten can morning"! I

would be so stuffed with cans in my pockets and jacket I probably looked like the 'tin man' in The Wizard of Oz.

Our formal bankruptcy was held at the Multnomah County Courthouse. Because of the size and anger of the creditors we'd been advised not to attend. We were to answer creditors, questions by phone; me in Warrenton, Kris in Hawaii. The creditors were so unruly they had to call in police to maintain control.

One of my companies was Bernu Premium Finance. Many private people deposited funds with us for a favorable interest rate. Consequently, I ended up being investigated by the F.B.I. and Securities Exchange Commission.

We'd spent over $100,000.00 in legal fees in our efforts to avoid bankruptcy. Most of our creditors were liquidated in the bankruptcy. However, some clever attorneys filed suit claiming 'misrepresentation' or 'civil' fraud. We'd run out of funds so couldn't defend these suits which meant that they were never discharged even to this day.

After 'divesting' or being divested from these enterprises my wife and I moved to the Astoria area where I assisted in the management of the Ford Dealership from 1984 through 2001. For over ten years I was featured on all our radio stations with 'A Thought for Today' an inspirational message. During this same period my wife and I took people salmon fishing out of Hammond, Oregon on the Pacific Ocean across the 'infamous' 'Columbia River Bar'.

The car business was a barrel of laughs. We had one Hispanic salesperson, a Finish salesperson and several Caucasians. On many occasions you'd hear a car deal being negotiated in Spanish, another in Finish and a third in English.

One day a 93-year-old lady came into test drive a new Escort and our Finish sales person was assisting her. She said after test driving the Escort "Eric I'm too old to buy a new car". Eric took her arm and felt her pulse and looked up with a big smile and said why you have the pulse and heart of a sixteen-year-old. The 93-year-old looked back with a smile and bought the new Escort.

On another occasion an older gentleman after testing a vehicle said "I'll buy it on one condition" "we have to seal the deal with a drink". We sent one of our people to the liquor store returning with a bottle and we sealed the deal with a drink.

A Return to the Sea

In 1994 I started a new adventure in Alaska. Serving as a captain and fishing guide at Yes Bay Lodge fifty miles North of Ketchikan. Everyday, at Yes Bay Lodge in Alaska was a new adventure. One time fishing for small rock fish with a father, mother and son (11) and daughter (8), I was dropping the baited line down when whambo bow! A 75# halibut hit. After quite a fight and boating the 'biggy', as I was putting the line down again 'bingo'! A 100# halibut hit the bait. After a real fight and getting the monster up to the boat, then there was no room in the 'fish well' for it so I lashed it to the stern of the boat and towed it to the dock.

On another, occasion fishing for halibut, what did we bring up but an 85# octopus. Then a 101# salmon shark hit and towed our boat around until the line finally parted.

Another time returning in treacherous weather from Bell Island with two elderly gentlemen we ran into 8' to 9' seas and blinding rain and wind. Just barely idling we were taking seas well over the top of the boat. At one point a crashing wave hit

with such force it knocked the windshield wiper off which made it almost impossible to see. As we approached the entrance to Yes Bay the seas started coming from every direction. The guests were really frightened, and it was quite a challenge for me, but we made it safely. Later the guests related the encounter to Bill Hack, the manager and said "Mr. Bernard saved our life" "we were both praying and reciting the rosary beads and all". It was just another day of adventure.

Reflecting back over the past few years we've (I've) experienced considerable pain and sorrow. The loss of our daughter Barbara, colon cancer, kidney stones, plus Cherie's blood condition, but also much joy. Family, get togethers at Thanksgiving, Christmas, Birthdays and Anniversaries. The great love and care our three remaining children show us, as I sit here writing and reflect back over almost 80 years. I have to say "Thank you Lord" for you have brought me through accidents, storms, financial difficulties, cancer and so much more. What a loving and caring God! "If God before us (and he is) who can be against us"? Praise your name! But it is not over yet. I plan to continue (the Lord willing) as a guide in

Alaska and seeking his guidance for the best use of my time the rest of the year.

I would offer this encouragement to all parents with teenagers. Don't give up hope on your kids. I was as bad as a kid could be but with the love and prayers of my mother and the loving grace of God I was 'changed'. Prayer does work and 'love never fails'

God is good!

Made in the USA
Monee, IL
08 October 2024

66998274R00046